SACRED
MASCULINE
SACRED
Feminine

ELIZABETH GRIEST

ISBN: 979-8-88615-184-8 (Paperback)
           979-8-88615-188-6 (E-book)

Inks and Bindings
888-290-5218
www.inksandbindings.com
orders@inksandbindings.com

Contents

Introductory Letter:

Dear Reader,

My thoughts/ feelings/ ponderings/ prayers on Sacred Masculine, Sacred Feminine help me.

I pray they'll help you.

Elizabeth Griest

I

One of the Greatest Mysteries of Life is the Existence of the Masculine, and the Existence of the Feminine.

II

Masculinity as well as Femininity are to be understood intellectually and empathetically.

So I believe.

III

Masculinity and Femininity are to be honored by one's head and one's heart.

So, I believe.

_____

_____

_____

_____

_____

_____

_____

_____

_____

_____

_____

_____

_____

_____

_____

_____

_____

_____

_____

_____

IV

The Masculine as well as the Feminine are Sacred because They Originate in Father/ Mother God of All.

_____

_____

_____

_____

_____

_____

_____

_____

_____

_____

_____

_____

_____

_____

_____

_____

_____

_____

_____

_____

V

The Sacred Masculine and Sacred Feminine originate from Father/ Mother God of All.

Thus, the Sacred Masculine as well as the Sacred Feminine are to be Revered.

_____

_____

_____

_____

_____

_____

_____

_____

_____

_____

_____

_____

_____

_____

_____

_____

_____

_____

_____

VI

To me, Sacred Masculine, as well as Sacred Feminine are Rooted in Sacred Simplexity – what's Simple, yet Complete.

Simplexity is <u>not</u> simplistic – Simple yet <u>In</u>complete.

_____

_____

_____

_____

_____

_____

_____

_____

_____

_____

_____

_____

_____

_____

_____

_____

_____

_____

_____

VII

I see Sacred Masculine Primarily as Firm Strength
Rooted in Kindness.

_____

_____

_____

_____

_____

_____

_____

_____

_____

_____

_____

_____

_____

_____

_____

_____

_____

_____

_____

_____

_____

VIII

I see Sacred Feminine Primarily as Soft Strength Rooted in Kindness.

IX

Sacred Parents of All, You Who are Our Father/
Mother, Bless us All with Your Sacred Masculinity.

_____

_____

_____

_____

_____

_____

_____

_____

_____

_____

_____

_____

_____

_____

_____

_____

_____

_____

_____

_____

_____

_____

X

Sacred Parents of All, Bless us all with Your Sacred Femininity.

XI

Sacred Parents of All, Bless us all with Your Divine Union of Your Sacred Masculinity and Your Sacred Femininity.

_____

_____

_____

_____

_____

_____

_____

_____

_____

_____

_____

_____

_____

_____

_____

_____

_____

_____

_____

_____

_____

_____

XII

I Believe Sacred Masculinity is Primarily Giver/
Receiver when United with Sacred Femininity.

_____

_____

_____

_____

_____

_____

_____

_____

_____

_____

_____

_____

_____

_____

_____

_____

_____

_____

_____

_____

_____

XIII

—◆◆❀❀◆◆—

I Believe Sacred Femininity is Primarily Receiver/
Giver when United with Sacred Masculinity.

XIV

Both The Sacred Masculine and The Sacred Feminine are first Receivers/ Givers with Sacred Parents of All.

_____
_____
_____
_____
_____
_____
_____
_____
_____
_____
_____
_____
_____
_____
_____
_____
_____
_____
_____
_____
_____

XV

Both The Sacred Masculine and The Sacred Feminine must first Receive their Divinely Designated Strengths from Divine Parents of All before there can be Balanced Expressions of those Strengths.

_____

_____

_____

_____

_____

_____

_____

_____

_____

_____

_____

_____

_____

_____

_____

_____

_____

_____

XVI

Relationships between men and women can – often do – become Unbalanced when the Sacred Balance of the Masculine and Feminine is not Honored.

_____

_____

_____

_____

_____

_____

_____

_____

_____

_____

_____

_____

_____

_____

_____

_____

_____

_____

_____

_____

_____

XVII

I Believe it's crucial for one's Inner Child to accept and cooperate with the Sacred Masculine and the Sacred Feminine to experience The Sacred Balance of the Masculine and Feminine.

_____

_____

_____

_____

_____

_____

_____

_____

_____

_____

_____

_____

_____

_____

_____

_____

_____

_____

_____

_____

XVIII

One's Inner Child holds one's deepest memories, attitudes about oneself and others – male and female; Life; God. As well as the Blue Print of one's Sacred Life Plan.

If one's Sacred Life Purpose involves a member of the opposite gender, then it's crucial for one's Inner Child to learn/ experience the Sacred Balance of the Genders.

XIX

I Believe it's wise to ask – even implore – Our Sacred Parents of All to help one's Inner Child accept and cooperate with the Sacred Balance of Masculine and Feminine.

_____

_____

_____

_____

_____

_____

_____

_____

_____

_____

_____

_____

_____

_____

_____

_____

_____

_____

XX

Further, I Believe it may well require Repeated/ Diligent Prayerful Effort to obtain one's Inner Child's acceptance as well as cooperation with the Sacred Balance of Masculine and Feminine.

_____

_____

_____

_____

_____

_____

_____

_____

_____

_____

_____

_____

_____

_____

_____

_____

_____

_____

_____

XXI

Sacred Parents of All, help my Inner Child and I recognize/ remember/ revere the Essentiality of the Sacred Balance of Masculine and Feminine.

_____

_____

_____

_____

_____

_____

_____

_____

_____

_____

_____

_____

_____

_____

_____

_____

_____

_____

XXII

I Believe it's Essential to recognize/ remember/ revere the Sacred Balance of Masculine and Feminine for one to fully live one's Divine Destiny.

One's Divine Destiny is what one is to live/ do that no one else can exactly live/ do.

XXIII

Divine Parents of All, help everyone live/ do his or her Divine Destiny via recognition/ remembrance/ reverance of the Divine Balance of the Masculine and Feminine.

_____

_____

_____

_____

_____

_____

_____

_____

_____

_____

_____

_____

_____

_____

_____

_____

_____

_____

_____

XXIV

Gratitude to You, Divine Parents of All for the Divine Balance of Masculine and Feminine.

XXV

Truly, I Believe, everyone's life would be far more
Blessed by living/ doing his or her Divine Destiny
through recognition/ remembrance/ reverance of
the Sacred Masculine and the Sacred Feminine.

_____

_____

_____

_____

_____

_____

_____

_____

_____

_____

_____

_____

_____

_____

_____

_____

_____

_____

XXVI

Truly, I Believe, the world would be far more Blessed through recognition/ remembrance/ reverance of the Sacred Masculine.

_____

_____

_____

_____

_____

_____

_____

_____

_____

_____

_____

_____

_____

_____

_____

_____

_____

_____

_____

_____

_____

XXVII

Truly, I Believe, the world would be far more Blessed through recognition/ remembrance/ reverance of the Sacred Feminine.

_____

_____

_____

_____

_____

_____

_____

_____

_____

_____

_____

_____

_____

_____

_____

_____

_____

_____

_____

_____

XXVIII

Truly, I Believe, the world would be far more Blessed by the recognition/ remembrance/ reverance of the Sacred Union of the Sacred Masculine and the Sacred Feminine.

_____

_____

_____

_____

_____

_____

_____

_____

_____

_____

_____

_____

_____

_____

_____

_____

_____

_____

_____